D1371815

# the liter is

# the liter is

## By Jerolyn Ann Nentl

Library of Congress Catalog Card Number: 76-24202. International Standard Book Number: 0-913940-46-1.

Design - Doris Woods and Randal M. Heise

There is much discussion regarding the spelling of meter and liter. Often you will see these words spelled metre and litre. The spellings come from the French language, the language in which the metric system was developed. The United States seems to prefer the -er spellings.

**Special Thanks to:**

Dr. Mary Kahrs - Professor of Education at Mankato
State University, Mankato, Minnesota

Mr. David L. Dye - Mathematics Consultant, St. Paul, Minnesota

**PHOTO CREDITS**

Mark Ahlstrom, Media House

R.M. Heise - Art Director

the
liter
is

Do you ever wonder how much of something there is in a container?

How much milk is in a carton? How much soda pop is in a can? How much gasoline will a tank truck hold? How much water will a waterbed hold? How much liquid is in a teaspoon or a tablespoon?

Finding the answers to those questions is not very hard to do using the metric system. It is not hard because the measurements used to find out "how much" are taken from the meter.

Do you remember from the book "THE METER IS" that the meter is the basic unit of measurement for distance?

When someone talks about "how much" there is of something, he is really talking about the volume or capacity of the container that is holding the "something."

For example: if your father wants to know how much milk there is in a carton he just bought, he is really asking what the volume or capacity of that carton is.

The basic measurement for volume in the metric system is the cubic meter. That is a box or cube that is one meter wide, one meter long and one meter deep.

Because the cubic meter is such a large box it is not a very useful unit of measurement. To make things easier, a small box that is only one decimeter wide, one decimeter long and one decimeter deep is used.

This is a cubic decimeter and it holds one LITER. If you filled it up with water, the amount of water you would have would be one liter.

# 1 CUBIC METER

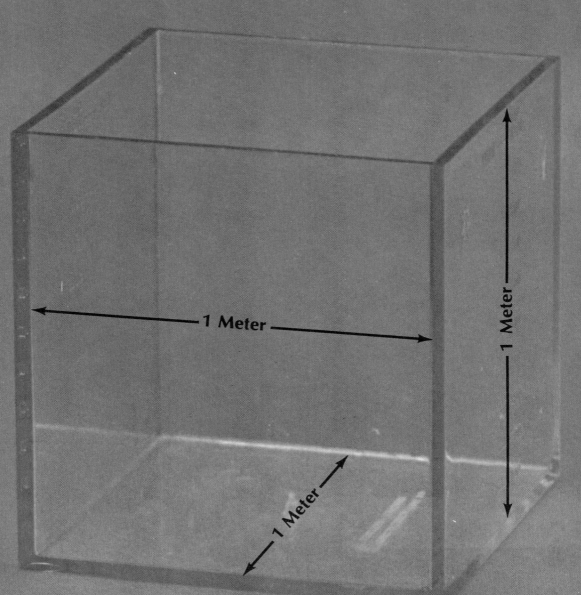

1 Meter

1 Meter

1 Meter

# 1 Cubic Decimeter = 1 LITER

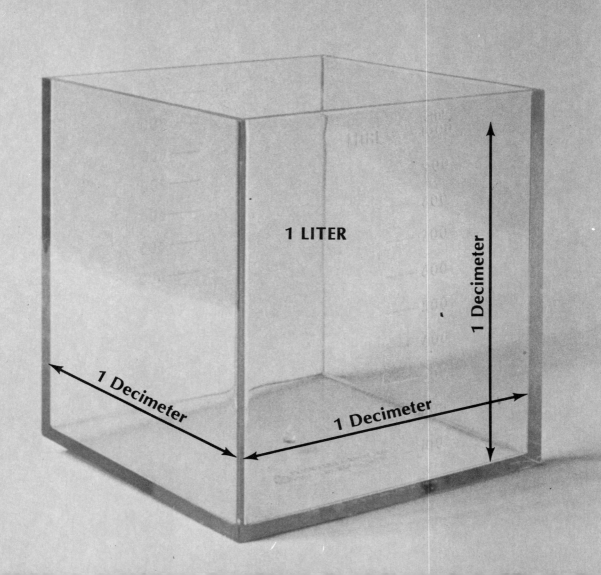

There are 1000 liters in a cubic meter.

We know this because a meter equals 10 decimeters. So a box that is equal to a cubic meter is also equal to a box that is 10 decimeters wide, 10 decimeters long and 10 decimeters deep.

Another way of saying this is that a cubic meter is 1000 times bigger than a liter.

# 1000 Cubic Centimeters = 1 LITER

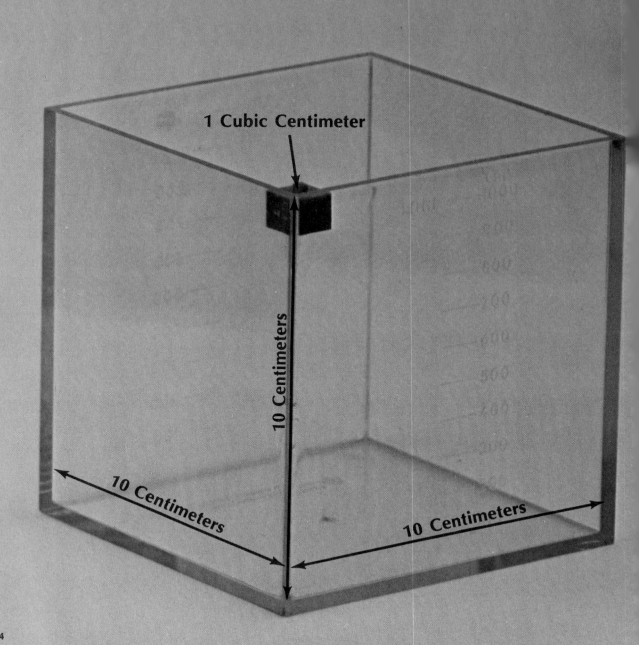

1 Cubic Centimeter

10 Centimeters

10 Centimeters

10 Centimeters

There is a third way of saying this: a liter is how much a box that is 10 centimeters wide, 10 centimeters long and 10 centimeters deep will hold. A box this size equals 1000 cubic centimeters.

Remember, the liter is used especially for measuring liquids.

The same prefixes are used with the liter as were used with the meter to show that there are 10 or 100 or 1000 liters or that there is 1/10 or 1/100 or 1/1000 of a liter.

**DEKA means 10.**

**HECTO means 100.**

**KILO means 1000.**

**There are 10 liters in a DEKAliter.**

**There are 100 liters in a HECTOliter.**

**There are 1000 liters in a KILOliter.**

DECI means 1/10.

CENTI means 1/100.

MILLI means 1/1000.


DECIliter means 1/10.

It takes 10 deciliters to make one liter.


CENTIliter means 1/100.

It takes 100 centiliters to make one liter.


MILLIliter means 1/1000.

It takes 1000 milliliters to make a liter.

You can make your own liter box by using the meter stick you made in the book, "THE METER IS."

On a piece of heavy paper or lightweight cardboard, make a drawing like the one on the next page.

Each square should be 10 centimeters high and 10 centimeters wide. In the drawing on page 19 the squares **are not** 10 centimeters.

To make sure your drawing is the correct size use the 10 centimeter scale below which is 1/10 of the meter stick.

**10 centimeters**

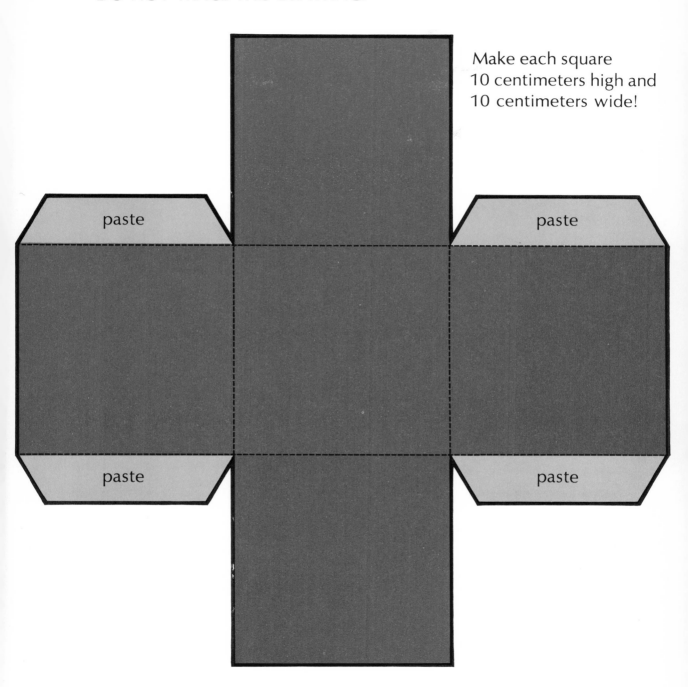

Make each square
10 centimeters high and
10 centimeters wide!

paste

paste

paste

paste

Remember to cut along the solid lines and fold along the dotted lines.

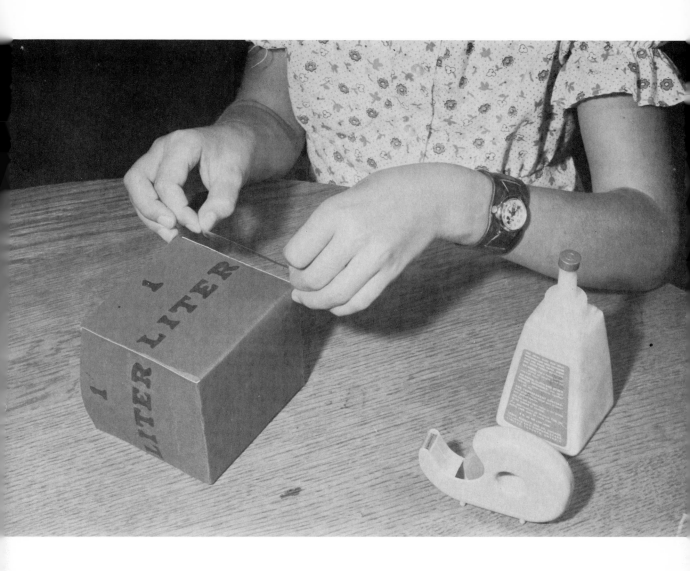

Put a small amount of glue on each flap to hold
the sides in place. Then fasten the box together with
tape.

Now that you have the box complete, use the 10 centimeter scale on page 18 to mark the outside of your liter box.

The centimeter markings will let you see about how much liquid volume things have.

Line the box with a small plastic bag to make it waterproof.

All the measurements you will make with your homemade liter box will not be exactly accurate. But the homemade liter box is a good way to get an idea of how much a liter really is.

Now let's try out the liter box. Start with something small. One teaspoonful of water will barely cover the bottom of the liter box because it equals only about five milliliters.

Two teaspoonfuls of water will equal only about 10 cubic centimeters or 10 milliliters. A tablespoonful of water equals about 15 milliliters.

Try a cup of water and see about how much it measures.

Now take an empty quart milk carton and fill it with water. Try it and see about how much it measures. It almost equals a liter, doesn't it?

To be sure, fill your liter box completely full with water and then very carefully try to pour all that water into the empty quart carton. A liter holds just a little more than a quart.

Find out how much liquid a coffee mug, a small teacup, a pop can or a flower vase will hold.

27

Larger things like the waterbed or the gasoline tank truck are too big to measure with the homemade liter box. Can you estimate how much they might hold?

A gasoline tank truck contains about 5 200 liters.

A waterbed holds about 650 liters.

The symbols for volume measurement are these:

| | |
|---|---|
| MILLIliter | - ml |
| CENTIliter | - cl |
| DECIliter | - dl |
| LITER | - l |
| DEKAliter | - dal |
| HECTOliter | - hl |
| KILOliter | - kl |

**Remember, the LITER is for measuring liquids.**

Now that you know about

# the liter

you should meet the rest of
the Metric family.

# the metric system is
# the meter is
# the gram is
# the celsius thermometer is

from